TAKING THE EGO LIGHTLY

Protecting Our Projections

THE PRACTICE OF *A COURSE IN MIRACLES*

TAKING THE EGO LIGHTLY

Protecting Our Projections

KENNETH WAPNICK, PH.D.

Foundation for A COURSE IN MIRACLES®

Foundation for A Course in Miracles®
41397 Buecking Drive • Temecula, CA 92590
www.facim.org

First printing, 2014
Printed in the United States of America

Library of Congress Cataloging-in-Publication Data

Wapnick, Kenneth, 1942-
Taking the ego lightly : protecting our projections / Kenneth Wapnick, Ph.D.
pages cm
ISBN 978-1-59142-749-0
1. Course in Miracles. 2. Ego (Psychology)--Religious aspects. I. Title.
BP605.C68W35995 2014
299'.93--dc23
2014034169

CONTENTS

APPENDIX

Dedication

We extend our deep gratitude and appreciation to Kathleen and Robert Draper for all of the help, support, and service they have given to the Foundation for more than 30 years.

We thank them as well for their dedication to Kenneth's work through their teaching in La Jolla, CA. They served as Directors of the La Jolla Branch of the Foundation from 1997 until its closing in August 2014.

Gloria Wapnick
September 2014

Preface

This book is an edited transcript of the seminar presented by Kenneth on August 17, 2013. It was the last class he taught before his illness and death. The original title of the program was "Protecting Our Projections," which was later modified for the published versions of both the audio and this book.*

As with all of the books in this series on the Practice of *A Course in Miracles*, the editing was intended only to enhance readability while preserving the informal, spontaneous feel of the class. With this in mind, we decided to indicate where there was audience laughter in response to Kenneth's characteristic humor and witticisms.

We have included an Appendix with an excerpt from a talk given by Kenneth in the opening session of a class from July 2013, entitled "The Community of Love." It movingly defines what his teaching throughout the years was all about, as well as the purpose of the Foundation, which he and I began in 1983.

As stated by Kenneth: "It is a community of love that exists in the mind, where people drop all their

---

* The audio is available in CD, Mp3, and Mp3 downloadable formats, item #191 at our Online Bookstore: www.facim.org. An e-book version will be available as well.

beliefs in separate interests, all their beliefs in ego thoughts of specialness and separation, and they become one with the music of this course."

And so are we urged to practice this principle as students, every day in every way possible! This diligence will speed us on our way to accepting the Atonement by helping us to awaken from this dream we are reviewing mentally. Hopefully, the importance of this goal is recognized and the love with which it is presented is accepted.

Rosemarie LoSasso
Gloria Wapnick

1. Introduction

The topic is "Protecting Our Projections." I know it sounds very dull and boring, but I'll try to enliven it a little for you. The phrase comes from "What Is Forgiveness?" in Part II of the workbook. This one-page summary has five paragraphs. Paragraphs 1, 4, and 5 talk about forgiveness; paragraphs 2 and 3 talk about an unforgiving thought. Here is paragraph 2 where the phrase occurs.

> An unforgiving thought is one which makes a judgment that it will not raise to doubt, although it is not true. The mind is closed, and will not be released. The thought protects projection, tightening its chains, so that distortions are more veiled and more obscure; less easily accessible to doubt, and further kept from reason. What can come between a fixed projection and the aim that it has chosen as its wanted goal? (W-pII.1.2)

What is clearly implied in this paragraph is the idea of *purpose*. The unforgiving thought is purposive. The attack thought, the expression of anger, has a purpose. It does not just come unbidden; it comes because it fulfills the purpose of making us mindless, as sentence 2 says: "The mind is closed, and will not be released." So the problem is never my mind's choice for the ego; the problem is out there in you. That is what the unforgiving thought does. "I am not the issue. Someone else, something made me angry. Something made me unforgiving. Something made me hold on to this grievance for decades." The unforgiving thought, then, makes it impossible to ever know that we are projecting. "The unforgiving thought protects projection" because I am now convinced, especially when I get people to agree with me, that *you* are the problem. The "you" could be a person alive or dead. It could be a public official, a head of state, the economy, the weather, etc. It could be your own body that is responsible for your illness or for your dis-ease.

The unforgiving thought "protects projection, tightening its chains, so that distortions are more veiled and more obscure. . . ." The purpose of projection is to keep the mind in prison. The mind then becomes enchained: "I'm so sure I'm right. *This* is why I'm upset." And, of course, we get people who agree with us, and it works perfectly. We are no longer aware that we are making this up. We are no longer aware, as Lesson 5 says, that "I am never upset for the reason I think" (W-pI.5). We think we are upset because . . . and we all have a *long* list of reasons that follow the "because." What the unforgiving thought protects, what the projection protects, is our mind's having made the wrong choice. Rather than deal with the guilt that inevitably ensues when we choose the ego over love, we say someone else is guilty. Rather than let go of the individuality and the personal self that the guilt ensures will always be there, we blame someone else. There are no exceptions to that. If you think there's an exception to that, you're thinking there's a world out there, a topic I'll get to shortly.

"The thought protects projection, tightening its chains, so that distortions are more veiled and more obscure; less easily accessible to doubt, and further kept from reason." We won't question the distortions. "How can you say I'm upset because I chose my ego? Look what this person's ego did! I'm *innocent*! Sure, I might have made a mistake or two, and maybe I shouldn't have quite said it the way I said it, but boy, if you knew what I've been through!" {LAUGHTER} And Heaven help the person who says, "No, I don't know; tell me what you've been through." {LAUGHTER} So never do that, all right!

In *A Course in Miracles* the term *reason* means right-minded thinking or the Holy Spirit's thinking, unless it's clear that it means "cause": this is why I did something.

"What can come between a fixed projection [that you are responsible for how I feel] and the aim that it [the mind] has chosen as its wanted goal?" Once I choose my goal to keep my individuality, which means to keep myself mindless, there is no way I am going to break the hold that I have on my projected object. That is why we sustain our anger and our grievances and why we are so sure we are right.

Now about the world, which I mentioned I would get to. One of the things that I always emphasize, as many of you know, is how important it is to understand the metaphysics of the Course. It is not *A Course in Miracles* if you do not recognize that the foundation of forgiveness, which is its central teaching, rests on the belief that the world is an illusion. What Jesus does in his course is go back and forth—sometimes even in the same sentence—between this metaphysical view of the illusory nature of the universe and the illusory nature of our individual projections, because they are the same. Thus, at the same time I tell people they really have to understand the metaphysics, I also tell people not to use the metaphysics as a reason for doing what they are doing: "I'm angry at this person because I know I'm really angry at God." Well, ultimately that's true, but that's just a way of not dealing with your anger. That is what I call "metaphysicalizing" or "metaphysics-schmetaphysics" {LAUGHTER} (you have to have grown up in Brooklyn to understand that!), where people use the metaphysics of the Course as a way of not doing the work.

Yes, it's true that in back of every object of anger and every projection is God. The Course says that over and over again, and while it is very important to understand the Course's theory—that's what you want to grow into as you go up the ladder—it is also really important not to use that as a way to avoid doing the daily work. That daily work is questioning not the original projection, which I will talk about, but your individual projections. It means truly looking at Lesson 5, "I am never upset for the reason I think" and applying that each and every time you become upset during the day. That is what it means to do the Course.

2. "The Substitute Reality"

What I want to do next is turn to some passages in the text that I don't usually cover, but that are relevant for our topic. First we will go to Chapter 18, section I. I often read paragraph 4, which I'm going to start with, but I want to continue and read paragraphs 5 and 6, and probably a couple of lines in paragraph 7. Maybe I'll read the whole section; I don't know. {LAUGHTER} Anyway, I will start with that because I want you to understand that the world is *the* projection and all of our little projections are found within that original projection.

I don't want to talk about the Course's view of time, other than to say there is no linear time, which means that the original projection is occurring right now, but *we* think it occurs when we project our guilt onto someone personally. That projection is just a fragmentary shadow of the original projection that we are all constantly doing. We are always making the world right now because there is no past. But again, you do not have to fully grasp that. What is important is to understand that that is the underpinning. That is why the Course says that when you totally forgive *one* person you have forgiven everyone (W-pI.108.5:2). It is always the same error.

We begin now with paragraph 4 of the section "The Substitute Reality":

(T-18.I.4:1-2) You who believe that God is fear made but one substitution. It has taken many forms, because it was the substitution of illusion for truth; of fragmentation for wholeness.

That is the original mistake of taking the *tiny, mad idea* seriously. Most of you are more than familiar with the line, "Into eternity, where all is one, there crept a tiny, mad idea, at which the Son of God remembered not to laugh" (T-27.VIII.6:2). The problem was not the thought of separation. The problem was we took it seriously, which meant in the original moment we listened to the wrong voice. We listened to the voice of the ego instead of to the Voice of the Holy Spirit. That is the problem. The ego never laughs unless it is a derisive laugh. The Holy Spirit laughs *only* because the original thought is so preposterously silly. How could part of perfect Oneness wrench itself from Oneness? Everything that followed from that, which is right in this instant, has to be preposterously silly also. So the Holy Spirit's response to everything, as is Jesus' response to everything, is always that sweet smile that says, "You're upset over nothing."

That, by the way, is how we know that the gospels were never written by anyone who really knew Jesus.

Nowhere does it ever say he laughed. Nowhere does it ever say he smiled. Read it! Read it in the original Greek, Hebrew, or Aramaic—you won't find it. Why? Because the writers of the gospels took the ego seriously. Therefore their Jesus had to be angry, anguished, and sad; he had to weep, to suffer, and to make people feel guilty, which unfortunately he did. He never smiled. That is how we know it is the wrong book. It may be the right book about the right ego person, but it is certainly the wrong book about the right person. So the problem at the beginning—this original substitution—was substituting the seriousness of the ego for the sweet, gentle smile of the Holy Spirit.

It was the substitution of seriousness—God and the separation thought are serious—for that sweet, gentle smile. It has been one error: listening to the wrong voice. That is the error. The error is not the separation. How could what never happened be an error? How could it be anything that you have to forgive? You forgive yourself for *thinking* it happened. The error is listening to the wrong voice.

(T-18.I.4:3) It has become so splintered and subdivided and divided again, over and over, that it is now almost impossible to perceive it once was one, and still is what it was.

No matter how many times the world has made itself over and over and over again and *is* making itself over and over again; no matter how many lifetimes you have come here (if you believe in past lifetimes) and made the same mistake over and over and over again, how many times in *this* lifetime you have made the same mistake over and over again, it still is the one error. You simply chose the wrong teacher. You chose the seriousness of the ego instead of that sweet, gentle smile of the Holy Spirit, and then once you projected your error, you believed the problem was out there. That is why the world is so serious. What is it that tells us the world is serious? How could a world of nothing—nothing projected as nothing—be serious? How could a dream that is made out of nothing be serious? (The dream is another major metaphor used in the Course.) How could a dream be serious? Its symbols may be serious because they remind you of something that never happened.

Why did we make the world so serious? What tells us it is serious? Our bodies! Our bodies have eyes and ears and all the other sensory organs that tell us about all the awful things that go on, the awful things that make us sick, that make us angry, that make us poor, that make us lonely, that make us feel hurt. Then we have a brain that we think has intelligence that takes all these data and brings them all together and says, "Ah, this means something. This is very serious."

All of this is a gigantic projection and is so convincing and so serious that we forget the single error, which is still there: we chose the wrong teacher, that one error that brought a smile to seriousness.

(T-18.I.4:4) That one error, which brought truth to illusion, infinity to time, and life to death, was all you ever made.

Everything else we ever made, from what we think of as the beginning of time to what we will one day think of as the end of time, is that one error. We took the *tiny, mad idea* of being separate from perfect Love seriously, made up a body to tell us how serious the mistake was, and instead of dancing gaily through the silliness of our life, we plod along—the Course talks about prisoners in chains, echoing Plato's Allegory of the Cave—never realizing the whole thing is a fiasco because we banished from our kingdom the one Person who would tell us that.

(T-18.I.4:5) Your whole world rests upon it [that one error, which is seriousness]**.**

It is not separation. What never happened cannot be the problem. That is really important to understand. Very serious things have happened to all of us in our lives as individuals, as members of national groups, racial groups, religious groups, social groups, and on and on and on. Very serious things have happened, and they are very serious if you look at them through the eyes of the body or through the eyes of the wrong teacher—the teacher of the holy frown instead of the Teacher of the holy smile. (I just used that for the first time, and you can use it if you would like to.) {Laughter} Everything rests on that. You can't fix a house that is falling apart if you don't fix the foundation. If you have a concrete foundation that has split, and the walls are now crooked and things are falling apart, nothing you do to the house will help if you don't fix the foundation. This is the foundation: choosing the wrong teacher. *Everything* rests on that.

(T-18.I.4:5-6) Your whole world rests upon it. Everything you see reflects it, and every special relationship that you have ever made is part of it.

The "it" is the original error. Everything our eyes see that seems so serious—or our denial of the seriousness by saying everything is wonderful and beautiful—reflects that original error. Every special relationship we have made, or are making now, or dream of making in the future, *every one* is a part of that original error, which means it is a shadowy fragment of the decision we are making right now. We all are making a decision right now as an ego, as a separated Son, to make the world real because we listened to the wrong voice.

The workbook tells us, "The world was made as an attack on God" (W-pII.3.2:1). That is a very serious statement, and it is true from the point of view of the ego. The ego *is* an attack on God. It is saying God's Love is not enough. Therefore the world that arose from it is an attack, but how could a world that does not exist be an attack on God? Only when you believe in the ego. That's why the sentence is there, and it is a very important sentence because it's a way of shooting all the air out of the ego's balloon that this is a wonderful world. "Let's bring peace to the wonderful world. Let's put an end to all sickness and make the world a wonderful place. Let's end all poverty and suffering. That's wonderful." And the Course says, "The world was made as an attack on God." It ain't going nowhere nice! {LAUGHTER}

You are not going to make this world beautiful, safe, or free from disease. The disease is guilt! You don't change the mind's guilt no matter how many vaccines or immunizations you get, or how many this or that; there will always be something. One of Freud's great contributions, as I've mentioned many times, was showing how our unconscious thoughts, our guilt, find their way to the surface—by hook or by crook they get out. That is what projection is. You have to get to the source of the projection.

(T-18.I.5:1-3) You may be surprised to hear how very different is reality from what you see. You do not realize the magnitude of that one error. It was so vast and so completely incredible…

What does "incredible" mean? It means it cannot be believed because it's not true. That is the error of taking seriously that preposterous thought: I am greater than God, I can find a love greater than what God has given me, and I can create greater than God. *A Course in Miracles* calls this *mis*create. Those of you who know Gnosticism will remember that one of the great Gnostic myths was the myth about Sophia, who was originally part of God's creation. Unfortunately, Sophia is a "she" in Greek. Also in Greek, "Sophia" means "wisdom." It's a kind of play on the word, though, because Sophia was not very wise; but men always like to make the error feminine, right? {Laughter} (I got a lot of agreement, at least from one gender in the audience.) {Laughter} Sophia thought she could create on her own like her father, and she did. She gave birth to the god who made the world, the biblical god. The afterbirth became the world. That is how the Gnostics thought of the world, as an afterbirth. You all know what an afterbirth is; it's not very nice {LAUGHTER}; it's a little bloody.

But Sophia thought she could create on her own. That's the error. That is not serious. It's just downright silly. God does not even know about it! But we know about it because we are the offspring of Sophia and Ialdabaoth. The name "Ialdabaoth" is the corruption of the Hebrew name for God, comparable to "Lord of Hosts." Ialdabaoth is Sophia's son. In fact, there's one very funny scene where Ialdabaoth—remember, this is the biblical god—is saying he is the great god, none greater than he. Then this female voice from the back says, "Whoa, just wait a minute. Remember who gave you life?"

Again, Sophia is the name for the error, what we would call the ego, of believing we could create like God. This wonderful universe of death, sickness, starvation, poverty, and suffering is our creation, and we think it's just wonderful. Remember what the biblical God says in the creation story in Genesis. He looked at all he created and said, "This is good; it's very good." Of course, the ego *is* very good. The ego says, "Look what I did. I'm greater than you, God, because I could kill what I created. You can't do that. So now I have power, not only over life, but over death too." That is the insanity of the world in which we live, and that is the insanity of the foundational thought of the world in which we live. The problem is not the world; it's not war, pestilence, sickness, or disease, or all the awful things people do to each other. True, all of that is awful, but it is not the problem. What is impossible is the *belief* in the impossible. That is the impossible.

Again:

(T-18.I.5:3) It [the error] **was so vast and so completely incredible that from it a world of total unreality *had* to emerge.**

From that original mistake of taking the *tiny, mad idea* seriously a world of total unreality had to emerge. That is what this world is: a place of total unreality. And look what we get upset about! If you are really honest with yourself you will look back and realize you got upset over nothing; at the same time you got upset over things you thought were of great magnitude. Things that upset you a day ago, a month ago, a year ago you now don't give another thought to.

We think things are so monstrously significant and important, and they very often *are* to bodies. So as I always ask, why do we stubbornly insist we are bodies and take seriously what we think are affronts, injustices, or calamities to us, when if we were to look right in back of us, we would see a little man, very sweet and very gentle, who keeps tapping us and saying, "Look, come, come, come listen to me. This is not what you think! Let me tell you a very funny story." {LAUGHTER} We don't want to hear a funny story, and so we say:

> "You don't understand; this is serious. It's not the time for funny stories!" {LAUGHTER}
>
> "No, but you've got to hear this little voice. It's really cute; it's sweet, it's funny, and it'll make you laugh."
>
> "No, no, this is too serious. I'm not letting go of my anger, or my grievance, or my pain, or my suffering, or my memories, or my specialness. No, no, no."

So poor Jesus just has to wait. He waits and he waits, but he's always smiling sweetly, gently, tenderly, kindly. That is what forgiveness means: you don't take things personally. You don't let things upset you. How could a world of total unreality upset you, unless you had an investment in the world of total unreality being reality? That is the problem. Our investment is that we want to be taken seriously. Our investment is we want the *tiny, mad idea*—me—to be taken seriously. God does not even know about us. Jesus smiles sweetly at all of our upsets and concerns. That is what this book is about. Don't be upset over nothing. Be grateful for everything.

We will come back to all this over and over again.

(T-18.I.5:4-6) What else could come of it? [What else but a world of total unreality could ever come from that original error?] **Its fragmented aspects are fearful enough, as you begin to look at them.** [Sure, war, pain, suffering, torture, sickness, death are frightening, and they make us fearful if we look at them.] **But nothing you have seen begins to show you the enormity of the original error, which seemed to cast you out of Heaven** [underline the word "seemed"!]**, to shatter knowledge into meaningless bits of disunited perceptions** [guess what that refers to?—everyone in this room, everyone in this world]**, and to force you to make further substitutions.**

Recall that the title of this section is "The Substitute Reality." It talks implicitly (not directly and explicitly) about all of our special relationships, which are substitutes. I say to God, "Your Love is not enough for me, but this person, this thing, this substance, this form of wealth is. This will make me happy. This will make me feel fulfilled, while Your Love does not." That is the substitution.

Nothing we have ever seen or thought or felt or experienced can begin to show us the enormity of the original error. It's enormous only in terms of what we *believe* happened. It is not enormous to God, to Jesus, or to the Holy Spirit, because nothing happened. To us, however, it is enormous. It literally made this whole universe, and it is still at this very instant making this universe. We insanely and stubbornly insist that this is the world and this is reality, and that all of our little problems, which may seem very large but in the end are very little, show us and should show Jesus, we think, how significant this world is. For now it is obvious that I am only talking metaphysically. We are going to leave all this behind later, but this is the backdrop for what really is important in this course, which is the daily practice of applying this idea in our daily lessons.

Again:

(T-18.I.5:6) But nothing you have seen begins to show you the enormity of the original error, which seemed to cast you out of Heaven, to shatter knowledge into meaningless bits of disunited perceptions, and to force you to make further substitutions.

In the workbook there is a line that says, "Another can be found" (W-pI.170.8:7). We will always find another special relationship, another grievance to make a story about, to build a case around. We will always find something.

(T-18.I.6:1-2) That was the first projection of error outward. The world arose to hide it, and became the screen on which it [the error] **was projected and drawn between you and the truth.**

The original error was the first projection of error outward. That is where we say the separation is not a thought system in *us*. The separation is *out there*. So the world arose to hide the error, because where is the error? The error is in the mind that chose the wrong teacher, that remembered not to laugh. That is the error. The "you" is the decision-making self that chose the ego. The truth is in our right minds where the Holy Spirit's gentle smile is that we chose against.

Again:

(T-18.I.6:2) The world arose to hide [the error]**, and became the screen on which** [the error] **was projected and drawn between you and the truth.**

In other words, *the unforgiving thought protects projection*. Thus, the problem is not what I have decided, namely, I have chosen against love. The problem is that the world, this person, this group chose against love, chose against *me*, and that's why I'm upset. But I'm protected from the truth that I did this to myself: "The secret of salvation is but this: that you are doing this unto yourself" (T-27.VIII.10:1). I now have no access to the truth because I'm so sure there's a world out there.

(T-18.I.6:3) For truth extends inward [it's in our mind]**, where the idea of loss is meaningless and only increase is conceivable.**

This is because love always increases. Earlier in the text Jesus discusses this. Ideas gain by being given away (T-5.III.2). This is not "increase" in terms of the world of time and space; it is not about magnitude. Love simply extends; that is what creation is, but not over time and space. It does not create another being; love just loves; that's all it does. It just loves. The idea of loss is meaningless. That is why Jesus is smiling. That is why we are asked to bring all of our problems and all of our tears to the holy instant where the Holy Spirit is, and where our laughter will be joined with His "gentle laughter" and our tears will be gone (see T-27.VIII.9). The problem is that we are not gentle, and when we *do* smile it is derisive or at someone else's expense. That's what jokes usually are.

What this course does and what we are talking about here just takes all the wind out of the ego's sails of projection. It just shoots them to hell—or to Heaven. *No projection is ever justified.* That is why he says "Anger is *never* justified" (T-30.VI.1:1; see also T-6.in.1; M-17.8:6). What happened in the 1950s and

1960s was awful in the long term. All of a sudden psychologists thought it was good for people to get angry. This was a reaction against what people misconceived psychoanalysis to be. People thought psychoanalysis was just about analyzing: analyze your anger and seek ways to express it. I remember there being T-groups, sensitivity groups, and all kinds of other groups back then. Then Gestalt psychology and Esalen took over. It was now good to express your anger. That might have been good for 15 seconds. {Laughter} I'm not for repression—that's never good; but anger is so sneaky because it feels so good.

The Course does not say, "Do not get angry." It just says not to justify anger. Don't say "I'm angry *because* of what was done." That's just an excuse. What's really going on is that I'm angry because I want to be angry at *you* rather than look at my guilt over telling Jesus to get lost, telling him that his love and God's Love are not enough—and that I want something more. We feel so guilty and are so fearful of punishment that we say, "I'm not the one who did it; *you* did it." The ego is always on the make, those beady eyes looking out always trying to find someone or something to blame. Then our anger is justified.

So "truth extends inward, where the idea of loss is meaningless," which means in the right mind. How could you lose love? How could you lose your Parent?

How could you lose perfect Oneness? If you could, it wouldn't be perfect Oneness anymore. That is the guilt, because if I exist, perfect Oneness cannot exist, which means in my warped insanity I believe I destroyed perfect Oneness because I exist; I am an individual. We project that out, "the first projection of error outward," and make up a world of fragmented little entities running around saying "I exist." And we're so sure we're right.

(T-18.I.6:4-5) Do you really think it strange that a world in which everything is backwards and upside down arose from this projection of error? It was inevitable.

This has a kind of double meaning. I remember being taught in high school science classes how an eye sees. The image cast on the retina is literally upside down. That's how the eye works. It takes the light rays from outside, the sensory data, and as they pass through the eyeball they cross, so the image on the retina is literally upside down. Very early on, obviously, we translate that. Our brain converts that original perception of an upside down world into something right side up so that we actually think we are all sitting here in chairs. We are really on the ceiling, somehow suspended, looking down. I am up there upside down talking to you. But our perception, what we experience, is that we are all sitting in chairs. This passage, in part, is a reference to that. It is really a play on the concept.

On another level, what this is really about is that everything here is backwards and upside down. It is all wrong because it is based on the upside down and backward thought that there could be something other than perfect Oneness and perfect Love. And not only that, but we *want* that "something other." That is why the only sane response to the *tiny, mad idea* is that sweet, gentle smile, that sweet silence that says, echoing King Lear, "Nothing will come of nothing." What is there to be upset about? Lear didn't mean it kindly at the time, but "nothing will come of nothing." This *tiny, mad idea* is nothing, and a world will inevitably arise from it, from nothing. Bodies will arise also as the fragmentation process goes on and on and splinters over and over again. So it is nothing fragmenting into nothing!

When you step back and understand this at least conceptually, you begin to realize why nothing ever works in this world, why there will never be peace in this world. I don't care how many peace conferences there are or how many treaties are signed. Doesn't anyone in Washington or any other capital in the world know this? Nothing will ever happen because "War begins in the minds of men," as the charter to

UNESCO says. *A Course in Miracles* refers to this as the war against ourselves (see for example, T-23.I.2:1; 4:1; 5:1). The title of Chapter 23 in the text is called "The War Against Yourself." We think it's a war against God, but since God does not know about it, how could there be a war? If there's only one party, how can there be a war?

(T-18.I.6:6) For truth brought to this could only remain within in quiet, and take no part in all the mad projection by which this world was made.

We bring truth to illusion, the opposite of healing. In the Course, healing means bringing illusion to truth. The best example of bringing truth to illusion is believing God entered the world, and in our Western world, without question, the best example is the Bible. The truth of God is brought into the illusion, and in the New Testament the *son* of God is brought into the illusion.

If you really understood this sentence, you would recognize how silly and how insane it is to think that Jesus knows anything about this world or that God knows anything about this world. It tells you right here: truth brought to this insanity, to this world of illusion, "could only remain within [in the mind] in quiet, and take no part at all in the mad projection by which this world was made," and which this world now is. So there is that little sweet, gentle man right here on our shoulder. Everyone has him. And we don't look. We don't want to hear his sweet, gentle, dulcet tone say, "Oh come on, it's such a funny story! Let me tell it to you. I'll tell it to you in any accent you want: Jewish, Italian, Japanese, French, Greek—any accent you want. I can tell you in *all* languages. It's a *very* funny story. Please let me tell it to you."

Our response is: "I'm too busy now taking care of the world. Sorry. {Laughter} Don't you know what's going on in the world? Don't you know what's going on in *my* world? I don't have time for your jokes. Hostile jokes that ridicule other people—I like those! I want to hear more of those. But the sweet—no, no, no; I'm not interested in that sweetness."

So, "truth brought to this could only remain within in quiet." Whom are you calling on when you ask Jesus, or God, or the Holy Spirit, or any other discarded entity you think is out there, to help you? Whom are you asking? You can't be asking him; not this guy. You're asking a projection. I've mentioned other times that many of the great Greek classics would end in a scene with a *deus ex machina* (God out of a machine). Things got so terrible on stage that there was no hope. All of a sudden a god descended in some kind of a machine—that's all they had in those days—and he made everything right.

Well, that's whom you're asking for help, some strange god in some strange contraption that is going to take him from truth into your world of illusion and fix things for you, so the audience will go away happy. Truth remains within, in quiet. Why does it say later on in the text, "The memory of God comes to the quiet mind" (T-23.I.1:1)? The memory of God comes to a *quiet* mind that is not always questioning, that is not beseeching, pleading, or angrily demanding. It comes to a quiet mind that says, "Please show me there's another way of reacting to this *tiny, mad idea.* Please show me there's another way of looking at the seeming seriousness of this world, of *my* world; the world of my loved ones. Please show me."

And all of a sudden this little man starts tapping on our shoulder again, and we ask, "Oh, is this really a funny joke?" He says, "It's the funniest thing you ever heard!" And we finally listen, and then guess what he says? He says, "It's a joke to think that time can come to circumvent eternity." That's what he says. And he starts laughing, and laughing, and laughing, and we say, "Huh? I think I missed something. Say that again?" {LAUGHTER} And so he says, "It's a joke to think that time can come to circumvent eternity, which *means* there is no time. Isn't that hilarious?" {LAUGHTER} "Ah, I'm sorry; go back to sleep," we reply. {LAUGHTER} And so he has to go back within quickly, because we don't want that answer. But that is his answer. You can read it right near the end of Chapter 27 (T-27.VIII.6:5). That's his answer; he's laughing!

And guess what? We don't want to join in his laughter because if we do, we would acknowledge that there is no time, and if there is no time there is no space, and if there is no space there is no world, and if there is no world there is no *me*! We don't like that one! So he just waits for another opening when we get fed up with the pain and the inherent futility of our lives.

Most of you know the wonderful lines near the end of *Macbeth*, when Macbeth's whole world has just collapsed around him and he knows the end is coming. He says, "It [life] is a tale told by an idiot, full of sound and fury, signifying nothing" (V,v). This is a world in which he killed; he drove his wife insane in order to gain the throne of Scotland, and he did attain it. Then he had to keep killing to keep the throne. At the end he realizes, "It is a tale told by an idiot, full of sound and fury, signifying nothing."

Shakespeare may not have known about the right mind, but he certainly knew what the wrong mind was. You certainly don't want to wait until you reach Macbeth's sad, sad state—to have your whole world collapse and your wife go insane and kill herself—

before you finally say, "Let me hear that joke again; maybe I'll get the punch line now." {LAUGHTER} Everything I'm telling you is true. That *is* what that little, little gentle, sweet man is saying. He is not hanging on the cross in seriousness. He is not saying, "My father, why did you let this happen to me? Why didst thou abandon me?" I mean, God! He is not weeping in agony in the garden. He is just sweetly smiling and saying, "Let me tell you a joke, guys."

Jesus is now talking about the error. I often read these next lines in classes:

(T-18.I.6:7) Call it not sin but madness [meaning *insanity*], **for such it was and so it still remains.**

How could you take insanity seriously, as a thought system? I'm not saying that you should dismiss people's pain, but how could you take what insane people say seriously? I've often said that while the clinical term is never used in this course, you can clearly recognize from many passages that the diagnosis of the separated son of God is *paranoid schizophrenia*. Unquestioned! Someone who is psychotic or schizophrenic has a thought disturbance that results in his seeing reality where it is not. The person hallucinates and is delusional, seeing things that aren't there, thinking things that are not true, and then believes the world is out to get him or her. That is the paranoia.

That is what Jesus is describing over and over again. Thus, Jesus is telling us not to call it sinful or serious. It's insanity! It was *always* insanity.

(T-18.I.6:8) Invest it not with guilt, for guilt implies it was accomplished in reality.

Well, it never happened, so how could you be guilty over what never happened? It is just a silly mistaken choice. You chose the wrong teacher. You chose the teacher of the holy frown instead of the Teacher of the holy smile. That is all you did! It is not sinful. There's no reason in the world to feel guilty. Guilt says, "I did something." A child steals and the parent says, "You should feel guilty because of what you've done. You're a bad boy or a bad girl." If you cheated on an exam, the teacher says, "You should feel guilty. Look what you did." Well, we didn't do anything. Nothing happened!

(T-18.I.6:9) And above all, *be not afraid of it.*

How could you be afraid of punishment for a sin you never committed?

All right, this closes the metaphysical idea. This is the foundation of this course and it really is important to understand it, *and then forget about it* {Laughter} because now I am going to read to you what you *should* remember.

•

3. Living the Teachings

"God Is Not Fear, but Love"

(T-18.I.7:1) When you seem to see some twisted form of the original error rising to frighten you, say only, "God is not fear, but Love," and it will disappear.

The "twisted form of the original error" is *any* special relationship we have with a person or a part of a person, with a sickness, a problem, a substance, an object, an idea, a cause, a past life, a future life. Any time you have an investment in *anything* and it rises up to frighten you, just say, "I just made the wrong choice. I just chose to believe that sin happened. I took it seriously and now believe God will punish me, and so I am justified in being afraid. Now I am justified in making a world, running out into the world, and believing that fear is all around me and is my justified punishment for what I have done. But if I remember that God is Love and that Love cannot be hurt, crucified, destroyed, fragmented, or substituted for, then the problem will disappear." That is what we have to know, because in back of this are those two workbook lessons I always mention—5 and 34: "I am never upset for the reason I think" (W-pI.5) and "I could see peace instead of this" (W-pI.34). That's what this is saying.

Note that the line says, "When you seem to see ..." because you are not seeing anything, just a projection of your own insanity. "When you seem to see some twisted form of the original error...." This wording takes the thought from a lofty metaphysical idea that we as one separated Son made the world, and it brings it down to me as a seemingly separated fragment of that insane Son. I have to pay attention to *this* individual fragment, not some lofty metaphysical principle that I don't really identify with. I will identify with it as I do my daily work. The "twisted form of the original error" refers to anything that you believe has power to threaten you and that you do not acknowledge is coming from your mind's mistaken choice. When this happens, you must quickly say to yourself, "God is not fear, but Love." "I am never upset for the reason I think" (W-pI.5). Our knee-jerk reaction *always* is to blame someone or something else.

I was mentioning to Gloria yesterday something that I remembered happening many, many years ago when we were in Roscoe, NY. I was alone in our house and I was walking from one part of the house to the other. No one else was in the house, and all of a sudden I felt a tremendous pain in my leg—it was almost as if someone had walloped me in the back of my ankle. I quickly turned around and my immediate thought was "Who did this?" My immediate thought! What happened was that I had pulled a muscle or something, but my immediate thought was, "Somebody kicked me in the back of my ankle"—that's how it felt. There was no one in the house. I *knew* no one was in the house. {LAUGHTER} Our kitten would not have done that, right? I knew Gloria was not in the house; Gloria wouldn't do it anyway, but I knew Gloria was not in the house. {LAUGHTER} But that's our knee-jerk reaction.

That's a cute example, but most of our examples are not cute. "Somebody did this to me!" Don't indulge it. Most of you have been with this course long enough now. Stop doing it! Stop with the baby business! "Peace to such foolishness!" (W-pI.190.4:1), the workbook says. Enough already! Stop with the blame! We're too advanced for this now. This is not nursery school; this is not written for kindergarten. Stop blaming! If I'm upset it's because my mind chose the wrong teacher. Now I'm being honest. And then Lesson 34 follows hard and fast on that: if I chose to believe God is fear and *not* Love, I can now choose to believe God is Love and *not* fear (T-18.I.7:1). "I could see peace instead of this" (W-pI.34) *right now*, and if I don't it is not because of my history. It is not because of how I have suffered in the past or because of what people have done to me in the past. *Right now* I am still too afraid of love and I don't want to hear that sweet, gentle man on my shoulder telling me his funny story because I heard it once and did not think it was very funny!

"I'm not a joke! Take me seriously, *damn it!* Take my anger seriously. Take my hurt seriously. I'm in pain. Don't you *know* that? Aren't you supposed to be Lord of all? Don't you know I'm in pain?" And he just smiles and says, "It's a *joke*! It's a joke!" And he laughs! In another context, St. Teresa of Avila is reported to have said to Jesus once, "That's why you have so few friends." {Laughter} She had accused him of pushing her into a stream. That's why nobody likes him. We bring such heavy stuff to him, and he just smiles sweetly and says, "I have a joke!" Again, it's right there near the end of Chapter 27. So that no one forgets about it, here it is: "Together, we can laugh them both away, and understand that time cannot intrude upon eternity" (T-27.VIII.6:4).

Jesus is saying to you and me, "I'm going to tell you a very funny story, so together, we can laugh them both away." (The "them" refers to the preceding sentence, that the separation happened and had real effects [T-27.VIII.6:3].) Separation cannot intrude upon perfect Oneness. "It is a *joke* to think it can." Now he's giggling, of all things!

"It is a joke to think that time can come to circumvent eternity, which *means* there is no time" (T-27.VIII.6:5).

Now what if you thought of that joke every time you were tempted to take the *tiny, mad idea* seriously? Just imagine what your life would be like if every time you were tempted to take something in your personal world or the world at large seriously you suddenly thought of that passage. "Together, we can laugh it away—it's a joke," he says. And then he's giggling, and you want to smack him. {LAUGHTER} You could smack him as much as you want. I tell you he will just keep giggling! You could build a brick wall around him and soundproof it, but he would still be giggling. It's sweet, soft, gentle, and tender, but he's giggling. Jesus loves alliteration: he giggles gently, tickles tenderly, and smiles sweetly. That's the real holy trinity. [Audience: oohs and aahs] You tickle your ego tenderly; you giggle gently at its insanity, and you sweetly smile at your seriousness in taking it so seriously. Remember that, and you will nevermore think of God, Christ, and the Holy Spirit—believe me—because They will disappear into that perfect Oneness, and you will too, with that gentle giggle. We don't want to hear that giggle. We want a Jesus who takes us seriously.

Once again, just read the New Testament, for God's sake, or for the ego's sake, or for whatever sake you want. Read it and you will see how serious it is. Forget about the Old Testament. There's nothing laughable in the Old Testament. There's nothing laughable in the New Testament either! In their arrogance, Christians think some of this is an improvement on the Old Testament. {LAUGHTER} Nobody laughs! Does God laugh? No. Read the Book of Job. It is Satan who is having a field day laughing. He makes a mockery of God as he destroys poor Job. This is a "holy" book. That is what is wrong with the Bible—it's serious. No one remembered to laugh. No one ever told a joke. No one ever told a joke *this* funny: "It is a joke to think that time can come to circumvent eternity." It is a joke to think that my seriousness and my specialness can overrule and overcome God's Love. That is a *joke.* It is not serious. It is not a sin. It is absurd and insane!

So, "When you seem to see some twisted form of the original error rising to frighten you, say only, 'God is not fear, but Love,' and it will disappear." Lesson 193 says twice, "*Forgive, and you will see this differently*" (W-pI.193.3:7; 5:1), and then at the end it says, "*I will forgive, and this will disappear*" (W-pI.193.13:3). It will disappear because I am remembering now to choose the right teacher. The problem is not the mad, cruel insanity that goes on in the world. It's *believing* in it. That is the problem, and we believe in the world because it protects the projection.

How many people, even *Course in Miracles* students, walk around every day and go through their daily lives remembering that they are projecting everything? I don't want you to go metaphysical on me: "Oh, I'm projecting this television set; I'm projecting this car; I'm projecting this 'this.'" No, you're projecting your *reaction*. That's what makes you a good *Course in Miracles* student. Otherwise, to say it once again, you are just indulging in *metaphysics-schmetaphysics*, and it means nothing. Yes, it is true that ultimately we are all projecting literally everything, but on a practical level that's nothing. You're skipping steps. I often tell people that this is not a pole-vaulting contest, where you go from the bottom of the ladder right to the top and it's important who can get there first. You have to go step by step. *Do the work!* The "work" is learning that you are projecting your *reaction*.

You have to understand the underlying metaphysics in order to understand why this is so healing, but I don't want you to think about it after that. You have to know the metaphysics if you are going to be involved with this course over a period of time. Whether you are learning it, teaching it, or living it, you have to know what it says. But if you don't *live* what it says it means nothing. I would much rather have a person who gets the metaphysics all upside down and backwards and is kind than a person who is intellectually brilliant and has mastered our famous chart and everything in this book but is unkind to everyone, or to even *one* person. All of that brilliance means nothing. *Be kind.* This course helps you to be kind. Another way of saying this is that the original error was our having chosen the teacher of unkindness rather than the teacher of kindness.

Stop with the fancy stuff. *Just be kind.* "God is not fear, but Love" (T-18.I.7:1). If God is Love (later on I'll read something else that makes the point), then *everyone* is loved because God is perfect Oneness. "God" is the synonym for perfect Oneness and perfect Love. He is not a person. He is not even a being. He is not anything that we can think of in this world. That's why the Course says you say "God is," and then you shut up. {Laughter} I'm sorry; it doesn't say that. It says: "We say 'God is,' and then we cease to speak" (W-pI.169.5:4). I was getting a little tired; I thought I would collapse it somewhat. {Laughter} What do you say after that? God is perfect "Is-ness" or perfect Being, but He is not *a being*. He is not an object or a thing. He is Love. He is Oneness. He is Eternity. Use any of those words you want to.

If God is Love, not fear, then everyone has to be part of that Love because that Love is synonymous with perfect Oneness. That is why anger is never justified, as we saw earlier (T-30.VI.1:1; M-17.8:6). That is why excuses to explain why you are angry or upset, or why you are this or that are never justified. Don't justify them anymore. We are out of kindergarten. This is not meant for kindergarten, grade school, high school, or even college. This is graduate work. It means you really have to *live* this and make no exceptions. If God is Love and not fear, *everyone* and every *thing* is part of that perfect Love because everything is a split-off part of perfect Oneness.

In a well-known passage from Chapter 28 (see T-28.IV.9), we are taught that a grain of sand is not holy; a book is not holy, a human being is not holy, a duck-billed platypus is not holy. {LAUGHTER} They are holy only insofar as they are projections of the Son of God, who is not a thing or a form, but a thought. A form is never holy. I'll bet no one ever thought of a duck-billed platypus as being part of the Sonship. Well, why not? "But they're extinct," you say? Nothing is extinct because nothing is ever *extant*, right? {LAUGHTER}

Once again, seeing "some twisted form of the original error rising to frighten you" means seeing this form as having power over you, or rising to attract you, because in the ego's world, love and fear are the same. Special love and special hate are the same. Pleasure and pain are the same. They are all part of the same coin that says separation is real and therefore I exist.

As I mentioned before, it would be helpful to read Lesson 193, one of the most important lessons in the workbook. It is all about forgiveness: "*I will forgive, and this will disappear*" (W-pI.193.13:3). This does not mean the object will disappear and my eyes won't see it. My eyes never saw it in the first place! It was not even there for my eyes to see (if my eyes could see). What disappears is my perception—my *mis*perception—that whatever I am seeing has power to affect me. We are all too old for this. Enough already with the silliness. "Peace to such foolishness!" (W-pI.190.4:1).

It is the height of self-indulgence to continually say, "Well, I'm still angry. I'm still in my ego. I'm still afraid." Yes, that's all true, but you could change! Why don't you change? And if you can't change, at least be honest and say, "I *am* upset. I believe I'm upset for the reason I think, and I choose *not* to see peace instead of this." That's all right. Jesus won't punish you—he will keep giggling. Enough already! Say that to yourself: Enough already! "When you seem to see some twisted form of the original error rising to frighten you,"—any object or anything you think has power over you and can make you happy or sad—"say only, 'God is not fear, but Love,' and it will disappear."

(T-18.I.7:2-5) The truth will save you. It has not left you, to go out into the mad world and so depart from you. Inward is sanity; insanity is outside you. You but believe it is the other way; that truth is outside, and error and guilt within.

That is the heart, the sum and substance of this whole course. We believe that error and guilt are in our minds because we believe we pulled off the impossible. We believe right now, at this moment, that we pulled off the impossible because we do not feel God's Love. That is what we have to recognize, because if we felt God's Love we would not be upset. If we joined in that gentle giggle of that holy man, who is just telling the joke over and over again, pleading with someone to listen, we would not be upset by *anything*, no matter what is going on around us. But as long as we believe that error and guilt are in our minds (meaning our wrong-minded ego), then we believe the truth is outside. Therefore, we just have to get rid of the bad guys and take care of the serious problem with our serious solution. Then, of course, we argue with people. "My serious solution is better than your serious solution." {Laughter} It doesn't matter *what* it is.

The truth is: "Inward is sanity; insanity is outside you." Why is insanity outside you? Because it is not *me*; what is *me* is the sanity of that gentle giggle that reminds me that perfect Love has never been compromised. "Not one note in Heaven's song [of Love] was missed" (T-26.V.5:4). Nothing happened! That's sanity. Thinking that I am a person, that I was born and will die, that I am a body interacting with other bodies, living in a world with a history, a present, and a future, and all kinds of other things—that's insane. I am still as God created me! Many of you know that the only lesson that is repeated more than once is "I am as God created me" (W-pI.94,110,162). He didn't create *me*—Ken—as a person. He created me as spirit, as an extension of His spirit, and it wasn't even that God *created.* God just *is*; Love just *is*. The "Is-ness" of Love is creation; everything else is made up.

"The truth will save you." This gentle man with this gentle giggle will save you because he will remind you to laugh at the *tiny, mad idea*, and he will tell the joke until one day you laugh with him. "It is a joke to think that time can come to circumvent eternity, which *means* there is no time." There is no space, no world, no specialness, no individuality, no problem. There is nothing. Then you will giggle; you will tickle your ego tenderly; you will giggle gently at Jesus' very funny joke; and you will sweetly smile at the seeming seriousness of the world in which you thought you once lived. Nothing would ever bother you.

(T-18.I.7:3) It [truth] **has not left you, to go out into the mad world and so depart from you.**

Nothing changed. You are just dreaming a horrid dream. *A Course in Miracles* talks about two dreams. There is the secret dream, which is the mind's insane belief that it separated from its Creator and Source. That is the dream of sin, guilt, and fear that Jesus referred to at the end of paragraph 6 in the section we are looking at here. Then there is the projection of the secret dream. This is the dream that there is a world. That is what protects the projection.

Thus, I don't know about a world in which there is a secret dream, where I am the sinner, believing I destroyed Heaven. I feel so guilty and believe I'll be destroyed as a consequence of my sin, which doesn't exist. The sinners are all *out there*! Or maybe *I am* the sinner, but the "I" is a body—a person, not a mind. So, first, this world is the projection, but my believing in it then protects the fact that it is a projection. Still, it is only a dream. Truth has not left me. It has not gone out into the world and departed from me or from you or from anyone else. It is there in the mind. We all have a right mind. The insanity is outside us.

We believe it is the other way around. We believe that the truth is that there is a world out there that impinges on us, that influences us, that affects us, and that intrudes on our peace. That is not true! I only believe it's true because I think I am "the home of evil, darkness and sin," as Lesson 93 says (W-pI.93.1:1), and therefore I deserve to be punished. I project that insane dream and then say *you* are the home of evil, darkness and sin. I know that I am afraid, but I tell myself that I deserve to be afraid because of what *you* are going to do to me, or what you have already done to me. However, if I say, "God is not fear, but Love," I disperse all these clouds of guilt. I undo the dream because I have undone its basic premise, which is that God is fear because I attacked Him. *There was no attack!* God is still Love and I am still part of that Love.

"The Alternative to Projection"

Now with this next set of passages, I will be reemphasizing what it means to *live* the metaphysical ideas of *A Course in Miracles*. We will begin with the section called "The Alternative to Projection" in Chapter 6 of the text. I don't usually read these paragraphs publicly, but they are very appropriate. We will start right at the beginning with paragraph 1.

(T-6.II.1:1) Any split in mind must involve a rejection of part of it, and this *is* the belief in separation.

Right at the beginning we believed we could split from the Mind of God. In the Course, when the word "Mind" is capitalized, it refers to the Mind of God or the Mind of Christ. In a few places it also refers to the Mind of the Holy Spirit. Then when we seem to have separated, there were now two minds: the Mind, which is the only truth, and the split or separated mind, the post-separation Son of God. The Course says that consciousness was the first split introduced into the mind after the separation and that consciousness is the domain of the ego (T-3.IV.2:1-2). Thus, in *A Course in Miracles*, consciousness is not a good thing. In New Age circles consciousness is the be-all and end-all—not in this book, though.

There is no consciousness in Heaven. Consciousness implies duality: you are conscious *of* something. There is no one in Heaven to be conscious of anyone else. There is only perfect Oneness and perfect Love and that is God. Once we believed we were separated, we became conscious. We believed we were conscious of a God from Whom we separated, Whom we now have made into an enemy, and on and on and on. That is the split. Ultimately, mind has split from Mind. When there is a split in mind, part of it is rejected.

However, once we have the separated mind, when we choose to join with the ego, the teacher of seriousness, we are rejecting the right mind, the home of the Holy Spirit, the Teacher of that gentle laugh. That is the belief in separation. So we continue to separate. Just as love extends and extends and extends, separation separates and separates and separates. Thus, we believe we separated from our Source; then we separate from part of our self: the wrong mind separates from the right mind. Then we separate from the wrong mind and make up a world. We make up billions and billions of fragments and separate each fragment from the other. So we are always separating.

Then we continue the charade of separation and fragmentation through projection. I continue to separate myself from other people by being angry at them, judging them, making them special love or special hate objects. We are continually separating and fragmenting because there is only one error. There is no time, and therefore we are always doing the same thing over and over again, which means we are always separating from that lovely, holy memory, the

Holy Spirit, that reminds us of the God from Whom we never truly separated. Once we think we're here, the problem is that we are separating from the right teacher and choosing the wrong one.

That is what this is talking about: "Any split in mind must involve a rejection of part of it [the mind], and this *is* the belief in separation." We believed, ultimately, that we separated from God's Love, and now we separate from the Holy Spirit's or Jesus' Love, which then means we will separate from everybody else because separation begets separation, begets separation, etc., etc.

(T-6.II.1:2) The Wholeness of God, which is His peace [also His reality]**, cannot be appreciated except by a whole mind that recognizes the Wholeness of God's creation.**

If you want to remember the Wholeness of God and that you are a *part* of that Wholeness, you must include everyone. That is what this is saying. You cannot begin to even appreciate, let alone experience, the Wholeness and loving Oneness of God unless your mind is whole, which means healed. Well, the only way your mind will be healed is if you see everyone here as the same, which means whenever you attack, whenever you say someone or something else is responsible for your lack of peace or disquiet, you are really saying, "I don't want to go anywhere near the Wholeness of God, and that little fellow with that joke. I don't want to be anywhere near *him*!" That is what you are saying each and every time you have an unkind thought. That is what you have to focus on, not the lofty metaphysics of this course; not its soaring non-duality. Challenge every unkind thought you have and bring it back to its source: your mind chose the wrong teacher. End of story!

If you did that religiously, deliberately, devotedly, and with great dedication over and over again, you would be done! You would be done with graduate school, post-graduate school, post-post-graduate school. You would be done! This means that when you cherish an unkind thought, justify it, and rationalize it, you are saying that you don't want to be done—you want to stay in kindergarten with the little babies. You don't want to hear Jesus' gentle, funny joke! {Laughter} You want to hear a joke that makes fun of the bully in your nursery school, or you want to hear a joke that makes fun of the teacher you don't like, or the principal who wears funny hats or whatever. As you grow a little older, then you want to hear a comedian make fun of the political person you don't like: "I really like that. That makes me laugh." What are you saying? "I don't want to hear that gentle man on my shoulder with his very inappropriate, unrecognizable joke." Yet, that's what would help you.

I began this class talking about *purpose*. There's a purpose behind unkindness: it keeps the dream going. It perpetuates the illusion that "I," this person I think I am, or whom I see in my mirror, is the "hero" of the dream (T-27.VIII) and everyone else is my enemy, unless I make that person an ally against my enemy, until the day comes when my ally now becomes my enemy. We all know the game. It just goes on and on and on.

Remember the line I quoted earlier: "The memory of God comes to the quiet mind" (T-23.I.1:1). If I don't want to remember Who God is and who I am as His true Son, I just keep my mind in a perpetual state of disquiet by forgetting I have a mind and then projecting the disquiet—or guilt, sin, and punishment—onto the world. Now I'm very happy; I'm miserable, absolutely miserable, but boy am I happy in my misery, which is why I never let it go! I love to always be in trouble. I love to always be having people do terrible things to me. I love to be always worried. An apple a day keeps the doctor away? Well, a grievance a day keeps that funny little man away, and he doesn't like apples, by the way. It reminds him of that "original sin" business. {LAUGHTER} He gets very upset about that. Don't tell him any apple jokes. He's not the one who called New York City "The Big Apple."

But that's what you're saying. That's what you have to hear—that to be unkind is a decision, an ongoing decision. Your misery and unhappiness is not caused by what that SOB did to you five minutes ago—it's *not*! There *is* no five minutes ago! It's *right now*. It's not what your abusive parents did to you 40, 50, or 60 years ago, or what 10 ex-spouses did to you, or what your ungrateful children or grandchildren did to you. It's a decision you are making *right now* to silence this funny joke that says there is no time, no space, and no individuality. That's what you have to see. If you don't see that, this whole course means absolutely nothing. It becomes, unfortunately, "full of sound and fury, signifying nothing" (*Macbeth* V,v). No matter how beautiful or how wise these words are, if you do not practice seeing the purpose behind your unkindness, this means nothing; *nothing*! Your years of study mean *nothing* if you are still indulging your unkindness. Just don't do it.

If you have an unkind thought, fine; you have an unkind thought. Just don't build a temple around it. Don't build an altar and worship it. Don't blame it on someone else! That's what this is saying. If you want to know the Wholeness of God, then you must know the wholeness of God's creation, which means seeing everyone here as the same. That is the precursor to remembering we are all one in Christ. We are all a perfect one, "a Oneness joined as One" (T-25.I.7:1). See the purpose without judging yourself or feeling guilty. Just realize you don't want to go home. You don't want to laugh at that joke. You want to stay within your own jokes. You want to stay within your own humor. You want to stay within your own serious world.

(T-6.II.1:3) By this recognition [of the Wholeness of God's creation, that we are all the same] **it knows its Creator.**

The mind will know its Creator. Remember, in *A Course in Miracles* the words "know" and "knowledge" are synonymous with "Heaven." The word "know" is contrasted often with "perception." Spirit knows; the ego perceives. When you see the word "know" ("it knows its Creator") remember that it does not mean an intellectual awareness. It means the *experience* of Oneness.

(T-6.II.1:4) Exclusion and separation are synonymous, as are separation and dissociation.

When we separate from God we exclude Him. When we separate from the Holy Spirit and Jesus we exclude Them. When we are angry at others or have a special love or hate relationship with them, we exclude them. So separation and exclusion are the same. We are choosing one over the other. Separation and dissociation are the same because when you dissociate you are not associating; you are *dis*associating. It is the negative of *associating*. Thus, instead of being associated with God, I now *dis*associate from Him. I am separate from Him. I say, "This is not a part of me." When I attack you, I'm saying, "You're not a part of me." Exclusion, separation, and dissociation are the same: "I don't want to be a part of you."

When I tell this gentle little man I'm not interested in giggling at his funny joke, I am disassociating from him. I'm saying, "I don't want you near me and I don't want your joke near me. It contaminates my very happy, miserable world. {Laughter} Don't take my misery away from me. I revel in it. I don't know who I would be without my misery, my sadness, my despair, my sense of futility, my anger, my abuse, my victimization. I don't know who I would be without my being a victimizer. Don't take it away from me." So I exclude him. I exclude his perception. I exclude his course. I separate and disassociate from it. Instead, I associate with my "friends."

There's that passage in the fourth obstacle to peace about our "friends." Who are they? Sin, guilt, fear, and death (T-19.IV-D.6). They are our "friends" to whom we run when we become afraid of love. We can throw in a few other "friends" as well: anger, grievances, specialness, etc. When you hear somebody expressing specialness, instead of attacking it, embrace the fear that's behind the specialness. That isn't too difficult. Don't attack it, don't judge it, don't change it, don't correct or criticize it. Embrace the fear that is behind the specialness. Tickle it tenderly, look at it gently, and giggle at the silliness of it. Smile sweetly at the person who is behaving so special. Stop making yourself separate from the specialness. Stop disassociating from it. Stop excluding the person by judging the specialness. Hear the pain and the fear behind it, and then remember that funny, funny joke: "It is a joke to think that time can come to circumvent [love]," which is the same as eternity.

It's a joke! Sure you're choosing specialness. Sure I think you're teaching the Course wrong. Sure I think you're reading the wrong spiritual book. All of that means *nothing*! It means you have brown eyes; I have blue eyes. So? You like chocolate ice cream; I like vanilla ice cream. So? Is that a sin? What's the big deal? We make it a big deal. That's why I always tell people not to hang around *Course in Miracles* students. There are lots of people out there you could have dinner with tonight—not the people in this room. {LAUGHTER} The only person I'm having dinner with tonight is Gloria. She is not a Course student; I am not a Course student, so we will be normal people, right? I'm only half-kidding.

Course people say, "Oh, that's specialness; you can't do that." They forget that every time they take a breath they are inhaling the air of specialness. They have a special relationship with oxygen, right? Are you going to condemn a person for that, or condemn yourself for looking in a mirror? So why are you making a hierarchy of specialness? That's what you have to think about.

Now this is also the main theme of this class:

(T-6.II.1:5) We have said before that the separation was and is dissociation, and that once it occurs projection becomes its main defense, or the device that keeps it going.

Why is projection separation's "main defense"? Because the unforgiving thought "protects projection" (W-pII.1.2:1-3). If you want to protect your separated state of being dissociated from God, excluding Him from your kingdom and your version of love, then you will project your guilt, your seeming sin. You will accuse other people of betraying God, excluding His Love, and choosing specialness instead of love. You protect the fact that you are projecting your guilt because you see it outside you. And you are so sure you're right.

Yes, everyone in this world is special. This book says it. What's the big surprise? We formed a special relationship with our ego right at the beginning. So? Why are you so surprised that people are special? Why are you surprised that Course students are special and indulge their specialness? What's the surprise? Does Jesus attack it? Does he condemn it? No, he gently giggles at it. He tells you a very funny joke. He's soft, he's sweet, he's tender, he's gentle. That's how he corrects—by his love, not by wagging a finger or quoting the Course chapter and verse.

Yes, people do reprehensible things. Of course! "Frightened people can be vicious" (T-3.I.4:2), the Course says. Well, everybody here walks around "uncertain, lonely, and in constant fear" (T-31.VIII.7:1). So? Hello. What's the surprise? So why do you single out certain people to be deserving of your anger, your hate, your accusations, your judgments, *your* specialness? If you want to know the Wholeness of God, know the wholeness of creation and perceive it. True perception precedes knowledge.

True perception, which is the same as "Christ's vision" is seeing everyone as the same. Therefore, if you want to remember knowledge and Who you are as part of God's living and loving Oneness, then see everyone as the same. That's the stepping-stone, the precursor, the prerequisite. When you don't see everyone as the same, it's because *you are afraid of love*; it is *not* because of another person. The other person is irrelevant.

Again: "once it [separation] occurs projection becomes its main defense, or the device that keeps it going" (T-6.II.1:5).

(T-6.II.1:6) The reason, however, may not be so obvious as you think.

(T-6.II.2:1-2) What you project you disown, and therefore do not believe is yours. You are excluding yourself by the very judgment that you are different from the one on whom you project.

This is not in iambic pentameter and does not have triple negatives. This is a straight declarative English sentence: "You are excluding yourself by the very judgment that you are different from the one on whom you project." That's your clue. That's why projection is such a powerful defense and keeps the separation going.

(T-6.II.2:3) Since you have also judged against what you project, you continue to attack it because you continue to keep it separated.

That's what projection is. There cannot be projection without judgment or anger: "you're the bad guy." We continue to project our guilt onto the other person because we continue to *want* to keep it separated. As long as I keep you separate from me *you* are the sinner and I am sinless and innocent. God will punish you instead of me.

We have to challenge every unkind thought, every judgmental thought, every thought that is based on the misperception that we are different from each other. We are *not* different. In form we are very different. Personalities are different; gender, height, weight, skin colors are different; preferences, nationalities, religions are different. Everything is different, but not on the level of the *mind*. So why do we make a big deal about differences? Because it keeps us in a mindless (i.e., body) state. That is the purpose. There is a purpose behind our maintaining our projections. That's what this is saying.

"You are excluding yourself by the very judgment that you are different from the one on whom you project." What am I excluding myself from? From the Love of God. "I am not the one," I say, "that excluded myself from the Love of God. *You* are! You are acting unloving towards me. Of course I have to retaliate. Of course I have to defend myself. Of course! I mean, look what you did to me! Look what you just said!" Or, "I have to protect this holy course from all these infidels who think the Course says God created the world." So they think that! Do you think God cares? Do you think Jesus cares? He's just by your shoulder giggling. Does that sound as if he's caring? So someone believes that. If the person wants to be corrected, by all means correct that person, but if he or she doesn't, then just let the person be happy. Who knows? Maybe in the end they're right and you're wrong. Maybe Jesus played a cosmic joke on all of us. {Laughter} I don't think that's so, but you can never tell.

Sure people have outlandish or outrageous ideas about what this course says. Let them. God doesn't care. Jesus doesn't care. I assure you, he's giggling! So why should you care? He's not asking you to defend his book. He's asking you to *live* it, not to defend it, not to proselytize it, not to teach it through your words. He's asking you to exemplify it, to demonstrate it, to be kind, to walk around this world with that Holy Trinity: gently giggling, tenderly tickling, and sweetly smiling at everyone and everything. You may not do it outwardly, but inwardly that is what he is asking, and if you remember him right over here on your shoulder telling you that joke, you can't help doing it. There's no way that you could let anything in this world bother you. That's what this is saying. This is Chapter 6, very early in the text. Again, this is not flowery speech. It's not difficult to understand.

Now Jesus continues:

(T-6.II.2:4) By doing this unconsciously [projecting onto others, keeping them separate, excluding yourself from love]**, you try to keep the fact that you attacked yourself out of awareness, and thus imagine that you have made yourself safe.**

This is the crux of the ego thought system, right here in Chapter 6. There is nothing about special relationships, no fancy stuff. That comes later. You are not aware that by attacking someone else you are attacking yourself. The fact that you continue to project and think you are so right keeps this unconscious, out of awareness, and keeps you in a perpetual state of mindlessness. If you are mindless, how are you going to change your mind? How are you going to change teachers if you are *mindless*? You can change teachers only by realizing you are a *mind*. You have to reverse the projection. You have to bring the projection back. That is what this is about, and the craziest thing of all is that we then imagine that we have made ourselves safe. Remember, this is all unconscious, so this course exposes what is unconscious.

Thus, rather than believe God or some external agent is going to punish me, I believe I've made myself safe because *you* are the guilty one. You will be punished! Why do we attack people? Why do we have to make people wrong even when they're wrong in form? Why do we *have* to make them wrong? If you do feel called upon to correct the form, do it kindly, lovingly, gently, sweetly, softly, without any investment in their taking your sage advice. By your defenseless behavior and kindness you are showing people there is another way. So sometimes you correct the form; sometimes you don't, because the form doesn't matter. It is love undoing the fear that matters.

Paragraph 3 makes the point even clearer.

(T-6.II.3:1) Yet projection will always hurt you.

We think it's hurting somebody else who deserves it, but projection hurts *you* because you have excluded yourself from love. Someone who is listening to that kind, gentle joke and feels the love of that joke and the love of that person telling you that joke can *never* hurt anybody else. You can *never* project; there's nothing to project! Instead, the love and the gentle laughter of that joke will simply extend through you. That's what heals. But when you exclude the love, when you exclude that gentle stranger with his wonderful sense of humor that you think is incredibly stupid and not funny, you are hurting yourself, and then you will project the source of your hurt, and you're off and running in the game of projection.

(T-6.II.3:2) It [projection] **reinforces your belief in your own split mind, and its only purpose** [the word "purpose" again] **is to keep the separation going.**

Remember, when we took the *tiny, mad idea* seriously and listened to the holy frown instead of the holy smile, we said, "I like being separated. I like being independent. I like being special. I like being on my own. I like being autonomous. I like being *right*." It behooves me as a good, healthy, strong ego to preserve myself. And how do I preserve myself? I keep myself mindless by splitting my wrong mind from my right mind, which I now exclude. I build a brick wall around that gentle giggle that infuriates me, and then I split off the projection of the split mind, fragment it, and project it out so that I become the good and you the bad. That's what this is talking about and what this course is saying. That is what the workbook is training our minds to think like.

The purpose of a separating, unkind, projecting thought is to keep the separation going. It is a thought system of sin, guilt, and fear alive and well. When we choose to be afraid over nothing, we are keeping the separation going. We are saying, "I'm not afraid because I think God is punishing me for my sin; I am afraid because of…." We all have our list of horrors, our catalog of monsters, our closet doors behind which we keep all these demons that threaten at any time to engulf us, but we are never afraid for the reason we think. We are not afraid of the monsters out there. They are all made up! Their purpose is to keep the separation going.

Think purpose. That is what you want to do every moment, with every thought and with every breath you take. *Think purpose*. What is the purpose of this thought, of this feeling, of these words I'm saying, of this behavior? What is the purpose? There can be only one of two purposes: to keep the separation going or to undo the separation. What keeps the separation going is to see everyone as different. What begins the process of undoing the separation is to see everyone as the same. So we next read:

(T-6.II.3:3) It [projection] **is solely a device of the ego to make you feel different from your brothers and separated from them.**

Clearly that is what projection does. I see you as more sinful than I am, or perhaps I see you as better than I am. I see you as different. Whenever we get angry, which is always projection, we are saying: You're different. You have done or said something wrong, something terrible. You have made me into this hateful, awful person. Before you came into my life, before you walked in this room, before you gave me birth, I was this wonderful, wonderful person! {LAUGHTER} I was such a happy thought-form. I was peaceful; I was radiant; I was romping around; I was so happy. And then somehow I got dragged into this sperm/egg business and out I came. Now I'm hateful, miserable, sick, upset, deformed—I'm this, I'm that. God! It's all your fault! You know, I was so happy before.

That sounds silly but it is a continuation of the same thinking that says what I am today is what you made of me 40 or 50 or 80 years ago, or yesterday. Near the end of the text, there's a line that tells us that whenever we are upset, we proclaim in some way: "I am the thing you made of me, and as you look on me, you stand condemned because of what I am" (T-31.V.5:3). I am the thing *you* made of me—this miserable wretch of a creature you see before you—and God will punish you because of what you did to me. Look at me! I'm a poor, miserable wretch, the scum of the earth, a scurvy worm. I can't do anything. I can't sustain a relationship or a job. I can't sustain being happy more than 20 seconds, and it's *your* fault, whoever the "you" is that you are blaming. The point is that you see the other person as different.

What is the correction? Seeing everyone as the same. The word "same" doesn't appear here, but it is clearly implied. This is talking only about the ego.

You should just stop and think that whenever you start to get angry you are really saying, "I perceive you as different from me, and the differences I perceive make a difference." You have to challenge that. That's what honesty means in this course in terms of our daily practice. Be honest about what you're doing. No one is making you upset. No one is causing you to lose the Love and the peace of God. Just say it! Be honest!

Many of you have heard me say so often that you should run like hell when anybody says, "I'm going to be really honest with you." God! That's the most *dis*-honest thing anybody could say! What they're really saying is, "I'm justifying my projections onto you and you'd damn well better listen because I'm right!" {LAUGHTER} That's honesty? Maybe as the world sees it; maybe as your therapist sees it; but not as *A Course in Miracles* sees it, and not as that gentle little man with that very funny joke sees it. He doesn't see it that way. *Honesty means accepting total responsibility for what you are feeling, thinking, saying, and doing.* No one makes you do anything.

While it is true that people can make *bodies* do something, they cannot make you hate. They cannot make you be unforgiving. They cannot make you project. They cannot! Sure, they can do something to your body in this world. There's no question about that, but then, as I said earlier, why do you stubbornly insist you are a body? Why do you argue for it? You can say, "My body is hurt. My life has been ruined because of what you did. You broke into my house and stole $10,000 worth of jewelry. I'm $10,000 poorer now in jewelry, but not in love, not in peace. You didn't break into my heart. You didn't break into my mind. Yes, you broke into my house or my car or did something terrible to my business. Yes, you did that. So? You didn't break into my mind. You didn't take the Love and peace of God away from me." So what's the big deal? What's the beef? What am I complaining about? Yes, I complain—justifiably so—if I'm a body, and lots of people would agree with you, but that's part of the insanity. That's the "protecting your projections." They can't take the Love of God away from you, so what the hell are you complaining about? That's what you have to ask yourself.

Look in the mirror! I believe this course. I'm devoting my life to it. How, then, could I possibly say I'm upset because of what people did to my business, to my home, to my car, to my loved one, or to me? They didn't take my love away from me. They didn't take my peace away from me. They didn't take the power of my mind to choose to finally listen to that gentle, sweet man who just wants to tell me one funny story. That's all he asks for. He is not even telling me that I have to read the whole goddamn book—a thousand or so pages! {Laughter} I just have to listen to *one* joke. Nobody took that away from me. That is what you want to ask yourself. That's what this is saying. "It [projection] is solely a device of the ego to make you feel different from your brothers and separated from them." It keeps the dream of separation, exclusion, and dissociation going, but now we feel it's not our fault as a mind—it's someone else's.

(T-6.II.3:4) The ego justifies this on the grounds that it makes you seem "better" than they are, thus obscuring your equality with them still further.

That's how our projections get projected: "I'm right, you're wrong." Sometimes I get asked by people to please tell their *Course in Miracles* group they're wrong. What are they wrong about—the metaphysics, the theory, or the kindness? You want to prove you are a smarter, better Course student than they. You want to prove your inequality is justified. Once again, I assure you, I promise you Jesus doesn't care about what people do with this course. He would just like them to *live* it, to be more kind. God, that's all he cares about. He was the one who first coined the term *metaphysics-schmetaphysics*. {Laughter} He was not born where the Bible tells you he was born. He was born in Brooklyn, and I know where: in a small bagel store on Avenue J in Brooklyn. {LAUGHTER}

That is what he cares about, not that you mastered the non-duality of this course. You will learn to *live* the non-duality of this course by being kind to everyone and everything. Never say there is nothing you won't do. Never say that. There's *everything* you would do if *love* is guiding you, if you remember to laugh at the absurdity that anything could circumvent God's Love. Recall the prayer in Lesson 189:

> Empty your mind of everything it thinks is either true or false, or good or bad, of every thought it judges worthy, and all the ideas of which it is ashamed. Hold onto nothing.... Forget this world, forget this course, and come with wholly empty hands unto your God (W-pI.189.7:2-3,5).

What empties your hands is not mastering the metaphysics. What empties your hands is universal kindness and seeing everyone as the same. That's what this is saying.

(T-6.II.3:5) Projection and attack are inevitably related, because projection is always [always] **a means of justifying attack.**

Why do I have to justify my attack? So that I won't bear the brunt of my heinous sin of separating from love and excluding love from me, and then having to deal with God's punishment. So I attack you and justify it.

(T-6.II.3:6-7) Anger without projection is impossible. The ego uses projection only to destroy your perception of both yourself and your brothers.

What is the perception of both yourself and your brothers? That we are the same. We are one in Heaven but the same in the illusion. That is impossible, however, once you project. "The ego uses projection only to destroy your perception of both yourself and your brothers." Once again, whenever you start to project, whenever you start to have unkind thoughts, whenever you seek to exclude, remember the purpose. Now, of course you can't have dinner with everybody; you can't be married to everybody; you can't do everything with everybody, but don't exclude people in your mind by making up stories about them, building cases against them, getting other people to agree with you. You live this course by acts, thoughts, and feelings of simple kindness.

(T-6.II.3:8) The process [of projection] **begins by excluding something that exists in you but which you do not want, and leads directly to excluding you from your brothers.**

First I decide I don't want God in my life. I don't want His Love, His perfect Oneness in my life. I want *my* love. I want my special love. I don't want oneness; I want differentiation. I want separation. I want exclusion. Then I feel horrified by my guilt, so I don't want *that*. So I dissociate my guilt and say it's not in me. I project it out and then say it's in you.

Now we will hear the other side.

(T-6.II.12:1-2) The difference between the ego's projection and the Holy Spirit's extension is very simple. The ego projects to exclude, and therefore to deceive.

The deception is that you and I are different, that you are sinful and I am sin-*less*, that I am a better *Course in Miracles* student than you are. We're different, and the differences are significant and real.

(T-6.II.12:3) The Holy Spirit extends by recognizing Himself in every mind, and thus perceives them as one.

For us this means He perceives them as the same because we're not yet up to the point of literally knowing everyone as one. He sees Himself in every mind. He recognizes Himself in every mind. Thus, when someone attacks you or attacks your beloved Course, you want to recognize the Holy Spirit in their right minds and feel—not just intellectually know—but *feel* their fear of that Love, of that loving Presence that they are now disowning and excluding. They couldn't possibly attack if they were not afraid of Love. And maybe in the end they are not even attacking; maybe you only *want* to see them as attacking. It doesn't make any difference.

You don't have to know whether they are projecting or extending. You don't have to know if their misunderstanding of the Course is "an honest mistake" or is a deliberate attempt to sabotage the Course. You don't have to know that. All you have to know is that you want to extend the loving kindness of this sweet little man who still wants to tell you this funny joke, and wants *you* to tell this funny joke to everyone else. He is not the kind of comedian who wants the jokes only for himself. He *wants* his material to be stolen. He doesn't have a copyright on it. {Laughter} He wants it to be used by everyone.

By your very actions demonstrate the joke of thinking that "time can come to circumvent eternity," or that it can circumvent perfect Love and Oneness. He wants you to tell the joke and *live* the joke: How silly it is to believe that part of Heaven's song is missing because of what someone or something has done. But you cannot extend the joke until you hear it and believe it, and you won't hear it as long as you think you're right and he's wrong and his joke is not very funny. It's the funniest thing you could think of! Part of Love separating from itself and then declaring itself *God*? That's hilarious! What poor Sophia did is laughable. Sure, she tried to create like her father, so she gave birth to a monster and the afterbirth became the world. Yeah, all right. Funny, silly! God is *still* laughing! But we take it seriously and then condemn and judge. *Nothing* here is worth losing the peace of God over. I don't care what it is. *Nothing* is worth losing the peace of God over.

(T-6.II.12:3-4) The Holy Spirit extends by recognizing Himself in every mind, and thus perceives them as one. Nothing conflicts in this perception, because what the Holy Spirit perceives is all the same.

There's no conflict. There's no conflict between a true *Course in Miracles* student and a false one. There's no conflict between what someone says about the Course and what someone else who disagrees with it says. There's no conflict because the people are the *same*. Bodies disagree, brains disagree, eyes disagree on what they see. So? We make a big deal about *nothing*! You should read these lines every day before you go out into the world or even before you start thinking—or think you're thinking.

(T-6.II.12:5) Wherever He looks He sees Himself, and because He is united He offers the whole Kingdom always.

"Wherever He looks He sees Himself." In the end we will realize at the top of the ladder that *we are* the Holy Spirit. There is no separate entity out there. He is our true right-minded Self. So we want to grow into that vision, that perception so that we see the right mind in everyone, and anything that appears to be wrong-minded we see as a defense against the right mind. Is that a sin to be punished or a silly mistake to be joked about and laughed about kindly, sweetly, and gently?

That is the question we need to ask ourselves, instead of protecting our projections by insisting we're right. We keep the dream going that way. What we want to do is uproot the foundation of the secret dream. The foundation of that secret dream is that the impossible happened and that love can be separated from, excluded, disowned, compromised, and destroyed. That's laughable, not to egos or to bodies but to healed minds. What heals the mind is its sharing perception with the Holy Spirit. There's a section later in the text actually called "Sharing Perception with the Holy Spirit" (T-14.VII). In His perception everyone and everything is the same.

(T-6.II.12:6-8) This is the one message God gave to Him and for which He must speak, because that is what He is. The peace of God lies in that message, and so the peace of God lies in you. The great peace of the Kingdom shines in your mind forever, but it must shine outward to make you aware of it.

(Note that "God gave to Him" is a metaphor.)

I have spoken other times about the idea of *indirect learning*, which is discussed in Chapter 14 of the text (T-14.I.4,5). We are not ready to accept the love and peace in a mind that we don't know about. But as we remove the blocks by not protecting our projections, the love will automatically shine through and we will begin to see sameness instead of differences. And when we perceive differences and act on them we will catch it more quickly and will not indulge our mistake. We will simply say, "Yes, I'm angry. I'm this. I'm that. I'm upset, I'm giving people and things power over me. I don't have to do that anymore." But it must shine outward to make us aware of it, which means if we want to remember the Wholeness of God's Kingdom we have to see its reflection in this world. It is reflected in our seeing the sameness of God's Son. Just realize there is a purpose behind your projections and your anger. The purpose is: "I'm too afraid of this love."

(T-6.II.13:1) The Holy Spirit was given you with perfect impartiality, and only by recognizing Him impartially can you recognize Him at all.

What does "impartiality" mean? Actually, it's a play on words. "Impartial" is the negative of "partial." That's wholeness. But "impartiality" can also mean not seeing everyone in part. When you are before a judge, you want a judge who is impartial, who doesn't see parts and doesn't play favorites. The Holy Spirit doesn't play favorites. Either everyone has the Holy Spirit and the fear of His Love, or no one does.

Again, "The Holy Spirit was given you with perfect impartiality, and only by recognizing Him impartially [seeing Him in everyone] can you recognize Him at all." That is the question you want to ask when you jump on the ego's bandwagon and start criticizing, telling tales out of school, gossiping, starting rumors, believing rumors, sharing rumors, and feeling good about saying bad things about people. Just stop yourself and ask whether you are seeing the Holy Spirit in that person. When you enjoy a comedian making fun of someone or something that you don't like, ask yourself if you are seeing the Holy Spirit in the person who is being ridiculed. Obviously not, or you wouldn't be laughing.

One of Freud's little-known books—actually it is a very clever book—was one of his early ones (1905): *The Joke and Its Relation to the Unconscious*. Obviously a lot of the meaning is lost in translation, but he analyzed many, many jokes and showed how they really reflect the projection of unconscious conflict. It's a very good book. I'm sure it's much better in German because the full meaning of the jokes would come through better. But jokes are not funny ninety-nine percent of the time. *This* guy's joke is hilarious. {LAUGHTER} Trust me, this guy's joke right here by your shoulder is wonderful; it pokes fun at no one. There's no projection, no conflict, no pleasure principle involved, no seeking to resolve guilt by blaming other people. There's none of that! Freud was brilliant, but he didn't know about this guy on his shoulder. He would have written a totally different book then, of course, because there is only *one* real joke. That's a joke this gentle man wants us to listen to and to laugh at. That's the only real joke. Almost all other jokes are at someone's expense.

"Only by recognizing Him [the Holy Spirit] impartially [in everyone] can you recognize Him at all." Again, see the purpose in *not* seeing the Holy Spirit in everyone, because if you really saw the Holy Spirit in everyone, if you saw His Love in everyone, if you saw that memory of God's Love in everyone, if you saw this loving man with this very funny joke in everyone, then you could not possibly attack anyone. You would realize, just as Chapter 12 says, that every attack is an expression of fear and every fear is a call for the love that has been denied (see T-12.I.) That's your vision. That's how you would walk the world! No attack, no blame. Everyone is the same!

(T-6.II.13:2) The ego is legion, but the Holy Spirit is one.

We could translate that to say that the ego is different and sees everyone as different. The Holy Spirit is one and sees everyone as the same. Everyone is the same.

(T-6.II.13:3) No darkness abides anywhere in the Kingdom [in our kingdom everyone is in darkness]**, but your part is only to allow no darkness to abide in your own mind.**

I wish *every* Course student would underline this and put it everywhere. I know I say this about a lot of lines, but this is one of those lines. {LAUGHTER} Please, please memorize this, please. It's very easy: "...your part is only to allow no darkness to abide in your own mind." Now that's not hard to remember, right? *Your part is only to allow no darkness to abide in your own mind.* That's your job—not to correct the world, not to bring *A Course in Miracles* to every hotel and motel in the world {LAUGHTER}, not to be better than the Gideons, not to outdo them. Your job is *only to allow no darkness to abide in your own mind.* Well, what is darkness? Darkness is guilt, sin, and the belief in separation. It is the desire, the ongoing fervent desire to exclude God's Love, the searing wish to tell that gentle guy with that funny joke to get lost. That is the darkness. The very end of the text, the very last paragraph says, "…and not one spot of darkness still remains to hide the face of Christ from anyone" (T-31.VIII.12:5).

"Your part is only to allow no darkness to abide in your own mind." Don't worry about the darkness in the world. "There is no world!" (W-pI.132.6:2). Work on the darkness in your mind. When an unkind thought comes, when it gets beyond the thought to words, and unkind words utter forth leading to unkind behavior, stop yourself and say, "Why do I want to banish myself from the Kingdom of light? Why do I want to make my home in evil, darkness, and sin? Why don't I want to remember that 'Light and joy and peace abide in me' [W-pI.93]? Why don't I? And if I don't, as is abundantly clear I don't because of all these unkind thoughts, then why don't I at least be honest about it?"

In an earlier chapter Jesus says we must be very honest and hide nothing from each other (T-4.III.8:2). "Be honest with me. I'll make a deal with you," he says. "If you're honest with me about your ego I won't tell you the funny joke until you want me to." He always has a catch. "I won't hound you with the joke. Just bring to me all your unkind thoughts. That's all. Bring them to me. Be honest with me. Be honest with yourself!" Specialness is *not* the key to the Kingdom, not the real Kingdom. Specialness is the lock that bars you from the Kingdom. See everyone as the same. There are no bad guys in Christ's vision. I'm sorry. It's true. Believe it or not, there are no bad guys in Christ's vision; *no one, nada, nulla, niente, nothing, no one*. {Laughter} There are only people who express love or call for love. That's how everybody is the same.

(T-6.II.13:4-5) This alignment with light is unlimited, because it is in alignment with the light of the world. Each of us is the light of the world, and by joining our minds in this light we proclaim the Kingdom of God together and as one.

"Each of us is the light of the world"—not some of us, not many of us, not a few of us, but *each* of us. To join our minds really means accepting the fact that they are already joined. How do you join with a mind that is already one with yours? You have to remember that you're one with it. Projection stops you from doing that. The vision of *sameness* is what makes this happen. That's what ends the dream of the external world along with its source, the *secret dream*, in the mind. All of that is gone. At long last the ego's thought system is silenced, its place taken by that gentle laughter, by that soft, wonderful giggle at the silliness of the whole ego thought system.

There's a part of everyone in the world that wants that, and the way to get to it is by just being honest and not forcing anything on yourself. Just realize, "I don't want it because look how I'm acting, look how I'm writing, look how I'm speaking, look how I'm behaving, look how I'm thinking. It's not universal kindness or universal sameness, which means I am still afraid, but that's not a sin. Yet I can't know it's not a sin unless I look at it." We need that gentle little man to help us look—or any other symbol we wish to use—who does not take our world seriously, and who remembers that it's "a joke to think that time can come to circumvent eternity.

4. Ending the Dream

I want to end by reading two things. One is a poem of Helen's and the other is part of the prose poem, "The Gifts of God." But before I do that I want to talk about them. They're parallel. The poem, which I've read other times, is called "Conversion." It was written on Christmas Day, actually, and at the end of the poem there's a reference to Christmas. It's in three stanzas. We originally called the poem "Silences" because the first stanza talks about the ego, which really silences the Word of God. In *A Course in Miracles* the "Word of God" is always a synonym for Atonement, correction, or forgiveness, some aspect of the correction process. Stanzas 2 and 3 talk about the silence of the right mind, when the ego's thought system is silenced. Then we realize the conversion. It was Helen who had the idea that "Conversion" was a much better title to get from the first to the second stanza.

The poem talks about the ending of the dream. It contrasts the ego's world that silences, excludes, and disowns the Word of God. It begins: "There is a silence that betrays the Christ because the Word of God remains unheard." That's the purpose. The Word of God is the joke that this lovely, sweet man is trying to tell us. That is the Word of God. "It is a joke to think that time can come to circumvent eternity." It's a joke wherein we finally remember to laugh at the absurdity of the *tiny, mad idea* that a part of God could separate from itself. But we don't want to hear that because our existence began with not hearing that and instead taking the *tiny, mad idea* seriously. But then we finally hear the joke and begin to really laugh. That silences the ego, and that's what paragraphs 2 and 3 talk about. That's what undoes the dream.

The final stanza is another instance—this happens a few times in Helen's poems—where there is a joining together of Christmas and Easter. One line says, "The peace of God shines down upon a manger and a cross in equal silence." That's because they are both part of the dream. The fact that a holy Son of God, separate from all of us, could be born is part of the dream. That's specialness. The fact that salvation comes because the same child grows up and then suffers and dies for our sins is also part of the dream. Even if you see these events as holy, they are all events within the dream, so they all disappear. The poem continues, "Neither one will last. The dream of a beginning and an end can never touch God's Son. He seemed to take a human form and then he seemed to die. There is no death because there is no birth. The crucified is risen up to God." That's how the poem ends.

Another of Helen's poems, "The Star Form" written at Eastertime, ends by saying, "There was a cross but it has disappeared. There was a world but there is only God" (*The Gifts of God*, pp. 66-67). "There was a cross," which is everybody's life, "but it has disappeared. There was a world but there is only God." When we accept God's Love the world disappears because the dream that made the world is gone. The dream that *is* the world is gone. This poem is parallel to a part of "The Gifts of God." I'm not going to go into the story of it, but this prose poem, "The Gifts of God," was the last authentic thing (I think) Helen ever wrote down. It was in the early part of 1978. It began and ended as a series of messages to her, lasting over a period of three or four months.

I'm going to read two paragraphs that come at the end of the section called "The Ending of the Dream." While three and a half years passed between the poem "Conversion" and this, they are really saying the same thing without talking about the ego, except at the beginning. But it does talk about the end of the dream, and the key thing here is the use of the words *every, everything, all,* and *everyone*—that *everyone* has to be included in this awakening. It doesn't mean you have to wait for everyone else. It means in your mind everyone is included because there *is* no one else. You're no longer excluding, you're no longer disowning, you're no longer dissociating. All that's left is that gentle joke of that gentle man who says, "None of this happened. It was only a bad dream."

So again, what you want to do is live your daily life like this, otherwise it doesn't mean anything. You want to live with the truth of this poem and the message I'm going to read to you. You want to live it in terms of embracing everyone and realize when you *don't* embrace everyone by your unkind thoughts, feelings, words, and actions, it's because of your fear of that love, not anything else. And fear is not a sin. It is just a call to be undone by accepting the love that is given you.

Conversion

There is a silence that betrays the Christ
Because the Word of God remains unheard
By those in bitter need. Unspoken still
The Word salvation holds for them, and kept
Away their resurrection from a world
That is but hell and alien to God's Son.
Homeless they wander, nowhere finding peace,
Unknown, unknowing, blind in darkness, and
Unborn within the silence of the tomb.

There is a silence into which God's Word
Has poured an ancient meaning, and is still.

Nothing remains unsaid nor unreceived.
Strange dreams are washed in golden water from
The blazing silence of the peace of God,
And what was evil suddenly becomes
The gift of Christ to those who call on Him.
His final gift is nothing but a dream,
Yet in that single dream is dreaming done.

What seems to be a birth is but a step
From timelessness to time. The peace of God
Shines down upon a manger and a cross
In equal silence. Neither one will last.
The dream of a beginning and an end
Can never touch God's Son. He seemed to take
A human form and then he seemed to die.
There is no death because there is no birth.
The crucified is risen up to God.

(*The Gifts of God*, p. 61)

From "The Gifts of God" (Prose Poem):

There is a silence covering the world that was an ancient dream so long ago no one remembers now. Its time is done, and in the little space it seemed to own is nothingness. The dream has gone, and all its dreams of gifts have disappeared as well. The first dream has been seen and understood [as] merely an illusion of the fear on which the world was based. Beyond the dream, [and] reaching to everything, embracing all, creation and Creator still remain in perfect harmony and perfect love. This is beyond the gate at which we stand. And shall we stay to wait upon a dream?

Your holiness is mine, and mine is God's. Here is His gift, complete and undefiled. It is Himself He gives, and it is this that is the truth in you. How beautiful are you who stand beside me at the gate, and call with me that everyone may come and step aside from time. Put out your hand to touch eternity and disappear into its perfect rest. Here is the peace that God intended for the Son He loves. Enter with me and let its quietness cover the earth forever. It is done. Father, Your Voice has called us home at last: Gone is the dream. Awake, My child, in love.

(*The Gifts of God*, pp.122-23)

[Moments of silence]

Happy kindness. Do listen to that guy!

APPENDIX

“The Community of Love”

Excerpt from the Opening Session of the July 2013 Academy Class (Originally titled “The Wealth of the Indies”)

Kenneth Wapnick

(Slightly edited for ease of reading)

Before I start the class, I want to read a quote that was recently given to me. I’d never seen it before, and it is something I think I should read before every class I give. It is a wonderful way of summarizing the overriding purpose of our classes and workshops. It is a quote from Dietrich Fischer-Dieskau, who was probably the greatest singer of German *lieder* (songs) in the 20th century. He died last year. He was a brilliant, brilliant singer. During an interview for his 80th birthday a number of years ago, he spoke about the musical influences on him and said that the greatest influence was Wilhelm Fürtwangler, the great conductor, whom I’ve mentioned many times. This is what he said, speaking of Fürtwangler:

> He once said to me that the most important thing for a performing artist was to build up a community of love for the music with the audience so as to create one fellow feeling among so many

> people who have come from so many different places and feelings. I have lived with that ideal all my life as a performer.

I'm going to reread it now to you, making it personal to me:

> The most important thing for a teacher of *A Course in Miracles* is to build up a community of love for the Course with the audience, so as to create one fellow feeling among so many people who have come from so many different places and feelings. I have lived with that ideal all my life as a teacher.

I think this says very, very beautifully what the purpose of all these classes and workshops here is. Actually, it is the purpose for which Gloria and I started the Foundation many, many years ago. We believe, and I'm sure many of you do, too, that the Course is one of the most incredible spiritual documents that the world has ever seen. And while many, many people protest love for it, in order to truly love it, you really have to embrace it—not only it, but its source. If you don't identify the source as Jesus, then any symbol of unconditional ego-free love would do.

But that is the overriding purpose of everything. It is not the specific things I say or the specific things I read from the Course that is the purpose, but to have you leave with a deep appreciation of what this book really is. Many of you already have that experience; otherwise, you wouldn't be coming. Many of you have come over and over and over again. But it is very easy to take it for granted. You hear the same words, you hear the same themes, you hear the same passages without really letting them get inside of you.

The thing that was unique about Fürtwangler as a conductor was that every performance was like a new performance. It was like an organic living process. You didn't listen to a Beethoven symphony, which he might have memorized over and over again, and hear the same thing again. You were hearing it for the first time, because every time he conducted it he recreated the incredible genius and love that was in back of that music.

The same is true of this course. As many of you know, I've likened it many times to a great work of art, which means you come back to it over and over again, and each time you read it or hear things from it, you will hear them differently because you are not in the same place anymore. They no longer are words and concepts; they become a thought of love that is emblazoned on your heart. That is what the purpose of all these classes really is: to give you an experience of what this is like. In other words, it is the content behind the words.

I frequently quote Isaac Stern who said that the real music is the silence between the notes. And Gustav Mahler, who was a great conductor and composer, said that the real music is between the notes. Well, the heart of this course is between its words. It is not the words. You can memorize the words and understand them intellectually, but if you don't live them, nothing happens.

And so each time you pick up the book, or each time you hear something about this course, it should be a new experience for you, as though you are hearing it for the first time. When that no longer happens, then either you have fallen asleep or you don't need the Course anymore—you have "graduated."

The phrase, "a community of love for the music" or "a community of love for the Course" has nothing to do with people getting together as people, as persons. It is not a community as the word is usually used. It is a community of love that exists in the mind, where people drop all their beliefs in separate interests, all their beliefs in ego thoughts of specialness and separation, and they become one with the music of this course.

There is that wonderful passage in the text called "the forgotten song" (T-21.I), also referred to at the beginning of *The Song of Prayer* pamphlet as the song the Son sings to the Father and the Father sings to the

Son. It is just a poetic way of talking about the Oneness of love that unites all creation. In that section, Jesus says the notes of the song are nothing (T-21.I.7:1). It is not the notes. It is not the specifics. One could easily say that the words of this course are nothing. It is essential to get beyond the words to the real message, which is love, but not love in the specialness sense, the way the world presents it. The real heart of this course's message is that we are all one, and that no thought of differentiation, separation, or judgment should ever be tolerated. Not that we don't have such thoughts, but that when they come, you don't tolerate them; you don't get accustomed to them; you don't feel one with people who attack the people you don't like, or who like the people you like. You realize that everyone is the same.

There is that wonderful line in the text that I quote very, very often where Jesus says "Teach not that I died in vain. Teach rather that I did not die by demonstrating that I live in you" (T-11.VI.7:3-4). It's the demonstration. And the way you demonstrate what this course is about, the way you actually live out its principles of forgiveness is to let this course become a part of you, not as a book, not as a theory, not as a set of words, not as a group, but because it so infuses you that all ego thoughts have to disappear.

And so that's the overriding purpose of this class. There will be a lot of words. I will say a lot of things. You will say a lot of things. I will read things. But you really want to penetrate to the music behind the words or between the words. And that you can only do if you set your ego aside. You should try to be as ego-free as possible. Just give yourself to the music. In a sense, see this class as a great symphony, with disparate voices and different instruments all blending together into one harmonious whole.

There is that wonderful phrase in the Course that speaks of us all joining "the mighty chorus to the Love of God" (T-26.IV.6:3). And so this course is such a perfect embodiment in form of that Love. That Love is abstract, nonspecific. Whether or not you identify with Jesus as the first person of the Course, his love permeates everything. And that is part of the community of love. That is why you are really here: to remember that forgotten song.

INDEX OF REFERENCES TO *A COURSE IN MIRACLES*

text

text (continued)

text (continued)

workbook for students

workbook for students (continued)

manual for teachers

* * * * * * * * * *

The Gifts of God

Please see our Web site, *www.facim.org*, for a complete listing of publications and available translations. You may also write, or call our office for information:

Foundation for *A Course in Miracles*®
41397 Buecking Drive
Temecula, CA 92590
(951) 296-6261 • fax (951) 296-5455